THE
BLUFFER'S GUIDE TO
RELATIONSHIPS

MARK MASON

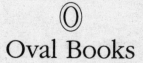

Oval Books

Published by Oval Books
335 Kennington Road
London SE11 4QE
United Kingdom

Telephone: +44 (0)20 7582 7123
Fax: +44 (0)20 7582 1022
E-mail: info@ovalbooks.com
Web site: www.ovalbooks.com

Published by Oval Books, 2004

Series Editor – Anne Tauté

Cover designer – Rob Oliver
Cover image: Digital Vision Ltd.
Printer – Cox & Wyman Ltd.
Producer – Oval Projects Ltd.

The Bluffer's® Guides series is based
on an original idea by Peter Wolfe.

ISBN-13: 978-1-903096-33-2
ISBN-10: 1-903096-33-2

CONTENTS

INTRODUCTION

In the old days, relationships were like the timer devices on video recorders – we all had them, but no-one knew how they worked. Boy met girl (or occasionally boy met boy) and that was the end of that. The couples would stroll off into the sunset, happy to have found each other. They'd never even heard of Oprah.

But now, in a world where the relationship is king, it is no longer enough simply to have a partner. The two of you must keep constant track of how healthy your relationship is, what it is founded upon and where it is going. Earnest discussions about your relationship are the very stuff of modern life. Not just with your partner, either. You're expected to talk about it with your friends, your family, your Ayurveda therapist, everyone.

In fact it could almost be said that love and companionship have become secondary aspects of the modern relationship. For many couples the main reason they're in a relationship is so that they can talk about being in a relationship. A situation is rapidly approaching where people have relationships with their relationships. Because of this, anyone wishing to take part in 21st-century social life has to be capable of talking Relationship. You must be familiar with the issues, the patterns, the theories. A hundred years ago you impressed people at parties by being an explorer. Fifty years ago it was being a nuclear scientist. Now you impress them by being a relationship expert.

Luckily the subject is custom-made for bluffing. Almost every survey, argument and piece of research about relationships has emanated from the same educational institution: the University of the Bleeding Obvious. Take Nahemow (pronounced Nah-he-moe) and Lawton, for instance. In 1975, these two academics undertook a study to determine how relationships began in the first place. They examined life in an apartment block, and found that the inhabitants were more likely to form relationships with ... people who lived on the same floor as they did. Your first reaction on reading this might be to bang your head against the nearest brick wall. But hold on a moment. This shows just what an easy subject 'relationships' is to master. Learn the basic theories, throw in the names of a few sociologists, and you'll be thought of as an authority in no time.

STATISTICS ABOUT RELATIONSHIPS

There is an old adage that one should use statistics like a drunk uses a lamppost: for support rather than illumination. Nowhere is this truer than in a discussion about relationships. They are elusive entities, hard to characterise, even harder to generalise about, and absolutely impossible to define to two decimal places.

Analysis of relationship trends is an art, not a science, so you must be prepared to indulge in some artistic use of statistics. For instance, take the claim that 'one in three marriages ends in divorce'. Or two in five, or whatever is the latest figure the press has headlined. Since this is the equivalent of saying that two in three marriages don't end in divorce, the statistic can just as easily be used to argue against the 'institution in crisis' theory as it can to support it. There will always be a variety of ways in which you can undermine the statistic itself. For instance:

Questioning the historical comparability of the statistic: "It was much harder to get divorced in the old days, so it's perfectly possible that a similar number of marriages would have ended in divorce at that time had the partners been able to obtain one."

Questioning the moral assumptions inherent in the statistic: "Just because a marriage continues does not mean it's correct to assume that it's a healthy marriage. The husband and wife may well be remaining together in a state of mutual loathing from which neither of them have the will or imagination to escape. As such, a marriage that ends in divorce need not be counted as a sad event, but a happy one."

Countering with reference to another relationship trend: "Many of the people who get divorced go on to get married again to someone else."

Employing flippancy: "The British Royal Family are skewing the figures upwards."

It should also be remembered that most statistics about relationships are even less reliable than the example above. The number of divorces in any particular year is both objective and a matter of public record. But the number of people who are, for instance, having affairs can only be estimated by conducting surveys. These are subject to hefty margins of error at the best of times, but when you ask people about their relationships there is the added problem of honesty. (Hence the well-known saying that there are lies, damned lies and statements about one's sex life.) In the case of infidelity, the fabrication could be in either direction; a vicar might be inclined to pretend that he isn't having an affair, while an accountant might be inclined to pretend that he is.

The seasoned bluffer can counter almost any relationship survey by casting doubt on the truthfulness of those questioned. To someone bemoaning the slack morals of today's teenagers, for instance, you can point out that it simply isn't the case that 74% of 16-year-olds have lost their virginity. The survey was wrong because of that curious creature known as the teenage male. If you ask a 16-year-old boy whether he's had sex, the answer will be "yes".

Another good way of devaluing statistics is by mocking the 'meaningless average'. A survey might have found that the average number of sexual partners in a lifetime is 12.4. Who was the point four? Danny de Vito?

8

The one subject about which you should know a few statistics is marriage. They are also good for diverting people if you're losing ground because, just as it is said that everyone loves a good wedding, it is equally true that everyone loves a good wedding statistic.

Highest marriage rate: The country that has more marriages than any other in the world is Antigua and Barbuda in the Caribbean. In 1999 the marriage rate was 22.1 per thousand population. On the other hand, the country with the *highest divorce rate* is the Maldives, with 10.97 per thousand inhabitants. From these two facts you can conclude that it's best to avoid important relationship decisions if you've spent too much time in the sun.

The most marriages: The female record-holder is Linda Essex of America, who has been married 23 times. The most marriages for a man is 29, by Glynn Wolfe, also of America. In June 1996, they married each other. Mr. Wolfe died the following year. When it was pointed out to his widow that the death had occurred only ten days before what would have been their first wedding anniversary, she replied: "What's a wedding anniversary?"

City with the most weddings: This is Las Vegas, which has more than 100 chapels performing 8,400 marriage ceremonies each month. This equates to one wedding every five minutes. There are plenty of people around the world who wish this was the standard duration of all weddings.

Longest wedding dress: In 2002 Jorian Schuit married Ernst Boekhorst in the Dutch village of Haastrecht. Her wedding dress was 2,545 feet long. The 250 guests helped carry it through the village after the ceremony, many of them making them calls on their mobile phones and saying 'Hi, I'm on the train.'

THE LIFE CYCLE OF A RELATIONSHIP

Much more powerful than statistics are facts. Especially surprising ones. As a bluffer you are well advised to keep a few of these up your sleeve in order to create the impression that you know far more than you really do. To bluff your way successfully in this subject, you must be aware of the basic theories about how relationships develop.

Kerckhoff and Davis' Filter Theory

This theory was first put forward in 1962. We know from the poet Philip Larkin that sexual intercourse didn't begin until 1963, so it's unclear how much relevance the theory can claim, but no matter. Kerckhoff, ignoring the fact that Davis's name wasn't nearly as geeky as his own and so wouldn't do much for his scientific credibility, studied lots of relationships to assess how they changed over time. Their conclusion was that there is a series of 'filters' through which relationships pass.

In chronological order these are:

1. The sociological filter
This is what determines whether the relationship ever starts in the first place. The group of people we meet is determined by sociological and demographic factors, and of course you can't begin a relationship with someone you've never met.

Kerckhoff's phrase for this group of people was the 'field of availables'. In the agricultural community the term can be taken literally.

2. The psychological filter

Kerckhoff and Davis found that couples who had been together for less than 18 months tended to have stronger relationships if their basic values were the same. In other words, if they agreed about fundamental matters such as standards of behaviour, having the same cultural frame of reference, sharing the opinion that her mother was not the devil incarnate, that sort of thing.

3. The complementarity filter

For couples who had been together for more than 18 months, the scientists found that agreement on basic values ceased to be such an important factor. Instead, longer-term couples had a stronger relationship if their emotional needs complemented each other. For example, a woman who felt a strong need to nurture would have a strong relationship with a man who enjoyed being nurtured. (N.B. this is not to be confused with the 'complimentarity' filter, where a relationship survived if the man regularly told his partner that her hair looked nice.)

The correct attitude to take when discussing the filter theory is one of amused cynicism. You can point out that it has completely missed some of the most important filters in an average relationship. For example the oil filter on the car. When a man forgets to change that, his relationship really is in trouble.

Thibaut and Kelly's Four-Stage Model (1959)

Published three years before the filter theory, this had one more stage. The four stages Thibaut (pronounced Tee-bow) and Kelly identified were as follows:

11

1. Sampling

In this early period, people investigate the costs and rewards of associating with different people in different ways, both by doing it themselves and by observing other people having relationships. (Note that this is not 'observing other people having relationships' in any literal sense. A magistrate is unlikely to be impressed by your defence that you and your binoculars were engaged in researching the first phase of Thibaut and Kelly's four-stage model.)

2. Bargaining

At the beginning of a relationship you give and take emotional rewards to establish whether it will be profitable for you. There is another type of bargaining, but this is connected with relationships of very short duration that tend to take place in hotel rooms.

3. Commitment

You cut down on the amount of sampling and bargaining in which you're engaged, and devote more of your attention to the relationship.

4. Institutionalisation

You settle down as a couple, establishing norms and expectations. If the relationship goes badly wrong, institutionalisation in a different sense may be called upon.

You will have noticed that Thibaut and Kelly's work paints an almost economic picture of relationships in which the partners act as self-interested dealers, treating emotions as commodities. This is entirely intentional. Most early work on relationships took this approach, which is known as 'social exchange theory'. It states that people assess the emotional pros and cons of becoming involved with someone with the aim of maximising their rewards in relation to their costs.

Warn others not to wait too long before choosing or they could fall into the 'conveyor belt' trap. This is the formula that assumes that of the people who come into your life randomly from the age of 16 to 60, you will want to pick the best item off the conveyor belt. But, as in a sushi bar, the longer you wait the more likely it is that the tastiest item will have gone by.

The optimum age for successful selection according to the academics is 32. But it sounds much more impressive if you use their equation: 'If 'e' is a mathematical constant whose value is about 2.7, you should choose a partner at the age of 'one over 'e'.'

A related lesson about choosing one's partner can be learned from the conveyor belts of airport luggage carousels: you must never walk off with someone else's property.

Homans' Principle of Satiation (1974)

Another proponent of social exchange theory, Homans argued that one of the most powerful of all relationship rewards is esteem. We are attracted to people who value us and our qualities. And, in particular, we operate on the 'principle of satiation'. Based on the traditional economic tenet that when something is in short supply its value rises, this contends that we will be especially attracted to someone who values a quality in us about which we are not ourselves confident.

For example, Pamela Anderson would be more attracted to someone who thought she was intelligent than to someone who thought she had large breasts. In the unlikely event that this ever happens, you now have the means to put Homans' theory to the test.

13

Murstein's Stimulus-Value-Role Theory (1976)

Bernard Murstein tells us that there are three different reasons for humans finding each other attractive. Most people, faced with guessing what they are, would answer "a mini-skirt", "a large bank balance" and "the consumption within the previous three hours of five double vodkas". And who knows, they may well be right. But Murstein, remember, was a sociologist, so his answers are rather more pedestrian. They are 'stimulus', 'value' and 'role':

- **Stimulus** is when the attraction is based on external attributes, such as physical appearance.

- **Value** is when it rests on a similarity of beliefs.

- **Role** is when the attraction depends on both partners successfully performing a role, for example 'husband' and 'wife'.

All three factors are present throughout a relationship, but the development of that relationship can be charted by their relative importance:

At the first contact between the two partners:
1. Stimulus
2. Value
3. Role

Contacts two to seven:
1. Value
2. Stimulus
3. Role

Contacts eight onwards:
1. Role
2. Value
3. Stimulus

If you want to agree with Murstein, you can point out that there are several aspects of his theory which fit with most people's anecdotal experience. For instance the declining importance of physical attraction as a relationship progresses towards long-term stability. If you want to disagree with him, you can say he should have stopped bothering about whether 'stimulus' was second or third, and got out more.

Sprecher's Self Disclosure (1987)

Self disclosure is seen by many experts as an important element in the development of relationships. Put simply, it means revealing things about yourself to your partner. A good name to throw into conversation if you're discussing this point is Sprecher (pronounced Sprecker). His work highlighted the 'ratchet' element of self disclosure. This refers not to one partner telling the truth solely because his girlfriend is applying a car mechanic's tool to strategic parts of his anatomy, but to the process whereby key points occur in the relationship when the level of self disclosure is ratcheted upwards.

For most of the time, both sides will match their rate of self disclosure to that of the other person. But once in a while an event may occur which suddenly reveals a lot more about one of the people in the relationship. At that point the other person will increase their degree of self disclosure to restore parity.

The nature of this event can vary widely. It might be the venturing of a controversial political opinion. It might be a reference to a hitherto unmentioned taste in a certain sort of music. Or it might be her getting home early from work to find him in fishnet tights and a red satin basque.

MAINTAINING A RELATIONSHIP

Being in a relationship is very similar to owning a car: maintenance is just as important as your initial choice of model. Once the early lust-fuelled attraction has worn off, you're faced with a whole lifetime (potentially) of important issues, all of which will require effort and teamwork. Like mortgages. Children. Coping with each other's snoring.

The means by which people maintain their relationships are, in the end, a matter for them. This hasn't, of course, stopped sociologists from persuading couples to spill the beans about them. Accordingly, familiarity with some of these studies could ensure your status for life.

Dindia and Baxter (1987)

(NB: You'll be noticing by now how often sociologists work in pairs. Rather like comedians, only less entertaining.)

In 1987, Dindia and Baxter interviewed each partner of 50 married couples, asking what strategies they used to maintain their relationship. Ranging from "talking about the day" through "paying each other compliments" to "spending time together with friends", there were in all 49 different strategies. If you are involved in a discussion where you want to paint an optimistic picture of the general state of human relationships, you can use this fact as evidence of a widespread reverence for the notion of staying together, combined with a determination to see that that is exactly what happens. If you want to strike a more pessimistic note, say that if something is in good condition you don't need 49 ways of holding it together.

One conclusion of Dindia and Baxter's study was that couples who had been married for a long time undertook fewer maintenance strategies than those who had wed relatively recently. This may have been because their marriages had matured and strengthened over the years, relieving them of the need to work quite so hard at keeping them healthy. Or it might just have been that they knew the game was up.

Brown and Harris (1976)

The 'social origins of depression' was the cheery subject of Brown and Harris's research. Their work highlights the importance of mutual support in the maintenance of relationships. They found that strong support at home could reduce the negative effects of stress in everyday life. Quite what you do when the person at home is the cause of your everyday stress wasn't spelled out.

Wellman (1985), on the other hand, showed that mutual support can sometimes have the opposite effect. He organised a group of volunteers to talk to other people for ten minutes about the most depressing thing that had happened to them recently. Another group were asked merely to think about their most depressing experience for ten minutes. At the end of the experiment, Wellman found that the talkers had undergone more negative mood changes than the thinkers.

The cynic would point to the apparent contradiction between Wellman's findings and those of Brown and Harris, offering the jaundiced opinion that sociologists will always find a piece of research to back up whatever theory they're advancing at the time. And the cynic would, of course, be absolutely correct. But the wily bluffer, instead of taking this as an indictment of the whole notion of expertise in relationships, realises that it provides the very key to becoming a relationship expert. Spend a few moments digesting the basic (if mutually defeating) theories, and you'll be armed with an argument for every occasion.

The craftiest of bluffers, indeed, can take this notion one stage further, and refer approvingly to both theories in the same evening. Although undeniably a high-risk strategy, it can be great fun, and you'd be surprised how often you can do it without anyone noticing, especially if your discussion is taking place in a pub.

Buunk and Hupka (1987)

The subject of Buunk (pronounced Boonk) and Hupka's study was sexual jealousy, and the effect it can have on a relationship. Their survey looked at 2,000 people in Hungary, Ireland, the Netherlands, Mexico, the Soviet Union, America and Yugoslavia. Their expense forms made for incredible reading.

They asked the interviewees to rate different activities engaged in by their partners, in terms of how jealous each one made them feel. The results showed a marked similarity between the sexes. The only differences were that women showed more jealousy about their partner kissing someone, while men were more jealous when it came to their partner expressing a sexual fantasy about someone else.

Neither men nor women were particularly jealous about their partner dancing with or hugging another person. This seems perfectly reasonable. Seeing your husband hug another woman is no great cause for alarm. It's the 'hug' he gives her in the stationery cupboard when he told you he was working late you need to worry about.

Yip (1999)

Andrew Yip's study looked at how couples in relationships managed the division between themselves of household tasks. Yip found that lesbian couples tended to share the tasks equally, whereas heterosexual couples organised the split along gender lines. Women, it was discovered, usually took charge of 'cooking', 'washing', 'ironing', 'cleaning', 'shopping', 'decorating' and 'paying domestic bills', while men would concentrate on 'confirming that the television set still works properly'.

THEORIES OF LOVE

Crucial to the study of relationships is the question of how one defines love. You will enjoy far greater success as you bluff your way in relationships if you can demonstrate a knowledge of this area, in much the same way that people would be more impressed with your bluffing about cars if you could show that you knew how a carburettor works. Fortunately, love is easier to understand than carburettors. Although when it goes wrong, it can be a good bit messier.

A useful opening statement when discussing this question is: "Psychologists and sociologists have studied love from a variety of angles." It doesn't really tell you that much, but if your audience snigger you'll know you've found their level.

Some psychologists think that 'love' is essentially the same as 'like'. In other words, that loving may be an extreme version of liking, but that its core qualities are the same. Others, however, think that it is qualitatively different. (A good word for the bluffer, that 'qualitatively'. It helps to lend a real air of expertise. Try and drop it casually into the conversation at dinner parties. But make sure you do so before the brandy, otherwise you've got no chance.)

Furthermore, there have been different theories of how love works, and indeed what love is:

Freud (1901)

Sigmund Freud believed that all emotions are inspired by the sexual drive we know as the 'libido'. This force, he argued, is life-affirming, but were we to go around wantonly indulging it, society would disapprove. We therefore use love, in the sense of being in a loving relationship, as a socially acceptable channel for our libido.

It is a good job for Freud that he died in 1939, because Warren Beatty was born in 1937, so if Freud had hung around much longer he'd have been forced to reconsider this theory.

Maslow (1954)

Love, argued Maslow (pronounced Maz-love – and with his name, who should know better?) can be divided into two types, 'D-love' and 'B-love':

D-love is 'deficiency love'. This is inspired by a person's insecurity in that they look to a partner to fulfil them and provide them with stability. Ultimately, according to Maslow, a relationship based on this sort of love is doomed to failure. Based as it is on a high degree of dependency, it will not be able to cope with the partner growing and changing.

B-love is 'being love'. This is a much more balanced kind of love, in which both partners are essentially secure in themselves. A relationship typified on B-love has a far higher chance of surviving, because both individuals' psychological needs are already fulfilled.

You may encounter references, particularly in the type of advertisement commonly found in newsagents' windows, to relationships involving the abbreviations 'O' and 'A'. These are of a quite different nature from the categories above, and should be passed over without further comment.

Lee (1976)

Not satisfied with Maslow's identification of two types of love, John Lee set to work and discovered six. Not only this, he described each of the six types as a 'colour'. Colours not in the conventional sense – red yellow, blue, and so on – but colours such as 'ludus, 'storge' and 'agape'. By learning the details of Lee's colours of love you will take a significant step forward in your bluffing:

Eros: this is where a person searches for a partner who fits a clear mental picture they have of their ideal physical type. It is very common, for instance, that a man will want a lover who has blonde hair. Especially if his wife is a brunette.

Ludus: the love in a relationship which both partners see as essentially light-hearted, rather than one which has a chance of leading to long-term commitment. Very popular on any number of Greek islands during the tourist season.

Storge ('stor-gay'): this is the type of love displayed in a friendship whose levels of intimacy and affection slowly increase.

Mania: a very intensive and emotional form of love, often typified by a person being possessive and jealous of their partner.

Agape ('ah-gah-pay'): a selfless, altruistic love in which the person looks after their partner and attends to their every need without expecting anything in return. Women are very familiar with this colour of love.

Pragma: a very calculating form of love. Someone experiencing this will attach just as much importance to their prospective partner's location or occupation as they do to feelings or emotions. A more common name for this type of love is 'gold-digging'.

Notice that when it comes to choosing names for colours, sociologists are every bit as pretentious as paint manufacturers.

Limerence (1979)

This is a term coined by Dorothy Tennov which refers to a very particular sort of love, namely infatuation which is passionate and all-consuming. Typical examples are Romeo and Juliet, Dante and Beatrice, Posh and Becks.

When gripped by limerence, people become obsessed by the object of their desire. They will often use tokens (photographs, gifts and so on) as a focus for their thoughts about that person. Their emotions will become intense, and take over their whole life. Restraining orders are not uncommon.

A key element of limerence, according to Tennov, is that the love is unrequited. If and when this situation changes, and a relationship begins, limerence disappears and the attraction becomes far less intense. Symptoms of this include a greater degree of rationality when dealing with the partner, a reduction in the need for physical proximity to them, and a tendency to wear socks in bed.

Limerence is commonly cited as an explanation for the intensity of teenage infatuations. Where a parent disapproves of the relationship and tries to prevent it, the teenager's feelings will become all the more powerful, which will in turn heighten their determination to act upon them. This can provide a useful lesson for parents. If you're worried about your offspring's infatuation with someone and wish to see it ended, resist the urge to ban them from seeing the partner in question. Instead you should ignore the issue. This may be difficult, particularly when the object of their affections has green hair, multiple facial piercings and a vocabulary that consists solely of grunts, but we are assured that the relationship will soon cease to be important to them, and their limerence will fade away.

Tennov was quite certain on this matter. And if you can't trust an academic, who can you trust?

Hendrick and Hendrick (1988)

(NB: Never refer to Hendrick and Hendrick as 'the Hendricks'. You will inadvertently label them with the name of the most famous rock guitarist ever, thereby giving sociology a level of street-cred it really doesn't deserve.)

Hendrick and Hendrick decided to study how people's views of love were affected when they were in love themselves. They asked 789 people whether they were in love. Sixty-three per cent replied 'yes'. (If you wish to introduce an especially world-weary note into your bluffing, you can add at this point: "The other 37% were married.")

They then used Lee's 'colours of love' to study their respondents' views about the subject. They found that those in love were more concerned with the erotic and agapic (selfless) aspects, while those not in love concentrated more on the ludic (short-term, light-hearted) features. This could be interpreted as proof of how seriously people take their relationships, of how much they realise that self-sacrifice and responsible behaviour are the key to long-term happiness. Or it could just be that the 37% were desperate for some action.

A useful by-product of Hendrick and Hendrick's work is that it allows those male bluffers with ulterior motives the perfect opportunity to progress. Approach an attractive female at a party. Engage her in conversation, and veer the talk towards relationships. Mention the 1988 study, asking in passing how she would have responded to the questions herself. If she replies 'not in love' and 'ludic', you're away.

Byrne's Formula for Love

A formula for love has, of course, been the Holy Grail of human happiness since time began. Most of us are happy to content ourselves with the tried and tested recipe of 'low lighting, three bottles of wine

24

and a Barry White album'. But Donn Byrne, being a sociologist, was determined to approach matters in a far more scientific manner. So he conducted interviews with respondents in North America, Britain and Holland, and came up with a formula that tells you whether or not you are in the 'throes of love'. The formula works by rating your feelings for a potential lover with those you have for an average friend and comparing the difference, using these five factors:

A: Your general attraction to the person. (On a scale of 1–10, calculate the strength of a particular friendship and compare it with your relationship – supposing that 5 means your missing the person considerably if absent.)

B: The intellectual stimulus you get when you are together (if a rating of 10 means finding the person's conversation vital).

C: Your willingness to be physically close (if 5 means you are on hugging terms).

D: The extent to which you want the person to want you (if 1 means it doesn't matter).

E: Your fear that your relationship with the person will break up (if 5 on the scale means you would be distressed if your friendship ended, but not devastated).

The idea is that if the score of your feelings for someone you think you love exceeds that for your friend to a sufficient degree, then it really is love. So, love is:

$(1.7 \times A) + (1.5 \times B) + (1.5 \times C) + (1.5 \times D) + (1.3 \times E).$

Sternberg's Triangular Theory of Love

Robert J. Sternberg tackled the subject by identifying what he saw as the three crucial components of love. These are:

Intimacy – This is defined by such features as promoting your partner's welfare; having a good mutual understanding; giving and receiving emotional support; establishing healthy two-way communication.

Passion – This equates to the satisfaction of your desires and needs. As well as sexual needs, Sternberg highlighted other needs, such as those concerning self-esteem and personal fulfilment. But stick to sexual needs. They're always good for grabbing people's attention.

Commitment – This measures how committed the partners are to their relationship, both in the short- and long-term.

Having established these three components, Sternberg went on to define different types of love depending on which components were present. 'Empty love', for example, is that where only commitment is present. If passion and commitment are both high but intimacy low, this is 'fatuous love'. The only way a relationship can survive, according to Sternberg, is if all three components are present. This is known as 'consummate love'. It is also known as a minor miracle.

Sternberg evaluated the incidence of each component by studying 80 men and women, who were aged between 17 and 69. Their average age was 31. (It might be argued that with an attention to statistical detail like this, Sternberg should have written about cricket not relationships.) He found that as the years go by, intimacy and commitment tend to grow, while passion tends to decline. Depending, that is, on how recently he has acquired a personal assistant. Or she has acquired a personal trainer.

Companionate and Passionate Love

Elaine Hatfield, writing in 1978, distinguished what she saw as the two basic types of love: passionate and companionate.

Passionate love is the sort we feel when we experience a deep, intense longing for someone. It is inspired by a biophysiological (you may have to practise that word) system which humans share with other primates. The emotions to which passionate love gives rise are very powerful; they can be wretchedly negative when love is not reciprocated, and blissfully positive when it is.

Companionate love is more akin to affection, the emotion felt between long-term partners who 'positively reinforce each other's intimate behaviours' (good phrase that).

Most people dream of combining the two types, that is to say, engaging in a relationship that offers the thrill of passionate love with the security of companionate love. But Hatfield is of the opinion that this may be impossible. A useful analogy here is with children at Christmas. Their passionate love for a present usually disappears very quickly. "Almost as soon," you might add with a glint in your eye, "as they've unwrapped it."

THEORIES ABOUT RELATIONSHIPS

So pervasive has the cult of Relationship become in modern life that relationship theories are springing up like weeds. Some authors who specialise in the sexual aspect of relationships have taken to calling themselves 'sexperts'. We cannot emphasise enough how important it is that you avoid using this word. Not only is it an offence against the English language, it will also give your bluffing a disturbingly populist feel.

Of course, the hours spent keeping abreast of the latest books on the subject could seriously reduce the time needed to establish a relationship. But, to be regarded as a master of the art, it is necessary to familiarise yourself with the most persuasive theories.

The doyen of modern relationship books is *Men are from Mars, Women are from Venus*. You might think it inadvisable to try to bluff your way about a book which so many people have bought. But have no fear. *Men are from Mars...* is like Stephen Hawking's *A Brief History of Time* and Marcel Proust's *A la recherche du temps perdu* – millions of people have bought it, but very few of them have got past page seven.

The vast majority of relationship hypotheses are aimed at those experiencing problems in their relationship or, at the very least, trying to prevent problems developing. And what most of them point out, in their different ways, is that almost all relationship problems are caused by one simple fact: men and women are different. Not a blindingly profound insight, you might think. But the forms in which the differences between the sexes express themselves are far more numerous and subtle than most people realise. Furthermore, they date back to the earliest days of the species, giving them a deep-rooted quality with which it is hard to argue. Take the time to learn these core facts about human nature, and your bluffing will reach new and hitherto-unimagined heights.

The Cave

Faced with a problem (about finance, work or whatever) women want to talk about it, while men prefer to retreat into themselves. Or, as relationship experts call it, into their 'cave'. Instead of discussing the problem with someone else they consider it on their own, silently brooding over possible solutions.

An alternative term for a man being in his cave is 'on the rock'. The plural of the term is where the relationship will be if the woman doesn't leave him alone at such times.

It is easy for women to misunderstand this taciturn behaviour. Because the man is not approaching them about the problem, they often think they must themselves be the cause. As a result they worry that there is some fundamental flaw in their relationship, so fundamental, in fact, that the man will be leaving them within weeks if not days, abandoning them to a future of uncertainty and loneliness. Whereas in fact the man is just trying to work out why Manchester United lost.

While the concept of a cave is merely emotional shorthand used by relationship writers, Native Americans take the word more literally. They believe that if a woman makes the mistake of following her man into his cave, she will be attacked by the dragon that guards it.

Another alternative term for the male habit of retreating into the cave is 'fire-gazing'. This has a similar derivation. When in the cave, the theory goes, prehistoric man would think about his problems while staring into the fire. Some experts believe that the modern equivalent is channel-flicking. Whereas women form an emotional bond with the television programme they are watching, men flick rapidly through the channels. It's something to stare at while they muse on their problems. Although it's surprising how soon the flicking stops if they stumble across a sports programme or a re-run of *Baywatch*.

Men Solve, Women Wallow

One of the most common mistakes that men make in relationships is to assume that women share their desire to solve a problem as quickly as possible, with the minimum of fuss. This is because when they were hunters, men had to hit moving targets so that the family could eat. As a result, the 'visual-spatial' area of their brains – the area which is geared towards problem-solving – developed far more than in women's brains.

This explains why a man will always seek the quickest and most logical solution to a problem, while a woman will enjoy the process of arriving at that solution, almost to the point of feeling cheated if the matter is dealt with too quickly.

So, for instance, when a couple are faced with the task of choosing new wallpaper for their sitting room, the woman will spend several days collecting as many sample books as she can lay her hands on, studying each and every sample in each and every book, imagining how that particular wallpaper would look in the room, evaluating every possibility to the nth degree.

The man will suggest papering the room with all the samples.

Men Are Literal, Women Are Emotional

This is another crucial difference between the sexes which has huge potential for causing relationship problems. It revolves around the communication of information between the two parties, and the different ways in which that information is processed. While men are inclined to give literal, factual and (most importantly, in their eyes) short answers to questions, women prefer what they would call a more imaginative approach. They will engage with the question on an almost emotional level, answering it in a sometimes roundabout manner, drawing in whatever thoughts it happens to trigger in their minds, no matter how tangential to the original enquiry.

Again, this is merely due to the different ways in which male and female brains are wired, but if the partners in a relationship are unaware of this, gulfs can occur. For example, she will ask him 'how was that drinks thing you went to with the people from work?' and he, because he thought it was O.K., will reply 'O.K.' She, being a woman, would have noticed what everyone present was wearing, who was friendly with whom, who was unfriendly with whom – in general the emotional temperature of the occasion as a whole.

So, if she had been answering the question, she would have given a detailed report. Thus when her partner replies 'O.K.' she doesn't think 'The drinks thing was O.K.', she thinks 'He's hiding something, I thought he was hiding something, I bet it's that new girl who's started in accounts, I didn't like the sound of her from the start, that must be it, he's having an affair with the new girl in accounts, oh my God what am I going to do, should I confront him about it now or should I have a talk with Cheryl first, I can't stand this, being rejected for the new girl from accounts.'

Men Are Mono, Women Are Multi

This is one of the most important ways in which the sexes differ. Men's brains are 'mono-tracked'. That is, they can only concentrate on one thing at a time. Women, in contrast, can split their attention, which enables them to perform several different activities simultaneously. A man will be unable to concentrate on a telephone call without lowering the volume of the television. A woman will have no difficulty in feeding a baby with one hand while she cooks the evening meal with the other, all the time reading an article in the magazine which is open on the kitchen table.

Or, to give another example, when her husband turns down the volume of the programme she's trying to watch because he's taken a phone call, she will easily be able to hit him over the head while she knees him in the groin.

Men Map, Women Picture

In prehistoric times, men ventured out to hunt for food while women stayed at home to look after the children and keep the cave tidy. As a result, the part of the brain that is responsible for direction-finding became much more highly developed in males than in females.

In terms of its potential to cause arguments in a relationship, this trait is unrivalled.

There is no way to eliminate completely the irritation which a man will feel at his partner's inability to follow directions, but there are ways that it can be reduced. For instance, when giving directions a man should remember not to use the language with which he feels comfortable himself, but to translate it into female-friendly terms.

Women tend to remember landmarks. So while he would naturally tell her "I'll meet you on the south side of Leicester Square" he should say "I'll meet you on the side of Leicester Square that faces the bronze statue of Charlie Chaplin".

The inability of the female brain to cope with directions was formally recognised in Britain in the mid-1990s when a publisher produced an inverted road map so that women driving south wouldn't have to turn the book upside down. On the day that news organisations broke this story, a faint breeze rustled through the trees up and down the country. It was the result of a million men simultaneously muttering 'Oh for God's sake'.

Men Are Strong, Women Are Loving

Men and women differ in the qualities which they value, and which will lead to them feeling secure in a relationship. Men tend to value strength, and want to feel needed, while women tend to value love, and want to feel loved.

So when it comes to deepening and strengthening a relationship, a woman will engage in such activities as making the home comfortable, preparing her partner's favourite meal, telling him on a repeated basis how much she loves him.

A man will bleed the radiators.

FREUD ON RELATIONSHIPS

The one person with a strong claim to having made a bigger contribution than anyone else to modern thinking about relationships is Sigmund Freud.

The great advantage Freud holds is that everyone has heard of him. They know that he is an acknowledged great in his field. So with your seemingly detailed knowledge of his findings, you will reflect some of that greatness on to yourself.

Before Freud, those who wrote about the subject were content to observe people's relationships and then describe what they had observed. Freud wanted to go further than this. His aim was to analyse people and the way they interacted with others, to explain why things happened in the manner they did. In so doing he generated an enormous amount of debate, revolutionised everyone's view of relationships, and founded the practice of psychoanalysis. But more important than any of this, he gave bluffers shedloads of things to bluff about.

The basis of Freud's thinking about how people relate to other people is to be found in his **Theory of the Self**. This states that everyone is made up of three distinct parts: the id, the ego and the super-ego.

The Id

The id is your unconscious part, the bit of you that operates on a purely instinctive basis, driven solely by your natural impulses and urges.

The Ego

This is the part of you that reacts to external reality, the section you're aware of, which you think of as the 'self'.

The Super-ego

This is your 'inner parent', the part of your mind that has been conditioned by good upbringing to moderate your behaviour, telling you what is and is not acceptable behaviour. It acts as your conscience.

When it comes to relationships with other people, problems arise because your super-ego is battling against your id. In other words, people have selfish, aggressive impulses that demand to be satisfied, but whose fulfilment would hurt others. For example, when out dining with a friend, you may remain hungry at the end of your meal. Your id, seeing that your friend is still eating, urges 'Don't bother about her, just push her out of the way and steal the rest of her food.' But your super-ego knows that this is entirely unacceptable, so prevents you from doing it. Thus is the problem of the id dealt with. Except in America, where the friends deal with it by ordering two meals each.

Freud said that the interplay between your id, ego and super-ego, and the conflicts in which it results, often cause anxieties. For instance the id allows a man, when he is under the influence of drink, to sleep with someone other than his wife. The next day, his super-ego takes over, making him feel guilty about the infidelity. In this way a new anxiety is born.

Most anxieties, according to Freud, are sexual. In fact most of everything in life, according to him, is sexual. But academics are allowed to get away with talk like that.

Unfortunately, these anxieties don't just go away like colds. Freud said that people have to find ways of dealing with them, or 'defence mechanisms'. Some defence mechanisms can affect one's relationships with others. These include:

Displacement

Whenever you repress an anxiety, its force has to go somewhere. Often this will be in the direction of someone else, and particularly someone close to you. Such an act is known as 'displacement'. An example of this with which most people will sympathise is that of the person who experiences a bad day at work and on returning home finds themself snapping at their partner. This is a common enough tendency for people to be understanding about it, as long as an apology is issued and it doesn't happen too often.

If not, use the aikido approach, the tactic of agreeing with criticism of oneself in order to neutralise it. The term derives from the martial art of the same name, wherein an opponent's strength is turned back on him. If your partner still doesn't stop criticising, try some aikido of the more conventional type.

Projection

This is when a person is unable to accept a failing in themself, and subconsciously projects that failing on to someone else. An example would be a domineering man who accuses his wife of being bossy. Or a lazy woman accusing her boyfriend of not working hard enough. Or Idi Amin accusing someone of killing his political opponents and eating them for dinner.

Should you have the misfortune to encounter a genuine expert in Freudian theory, you can escape from the situation by referring to Sigmund's wife Martha Bernays. She is on record as having insisted that in 53 years of marriage they never exchanged an angry word. Assuming she was telling the truth, you should say that Freud's personal experience of relationships was so untypical as to be worthless.

PROBLEMS IN STUDYING RELATIONSHIPS

Only rarely do sociologists admit that the study of human relationships is an inexact science, often categorised by flawed procedure and unreliable methods. Why they should be so reluctant to admit the faults of their profession is unclear. But when you give a person a clipboard and call him or her a sociologist, strange things happen. It's a good idea, therefore, to be aware of a few of those who have questioned their colleagues' work. Whenever you find yourself losing an argument you can throw in a reference to one of them, thereby whipping the intellectual rug from beneath your opponent's feet.

Huston and Levinger (1978)

Huston and Levinger pointed out that research into attraction had only studied three types of relationship: same-age, same-sex friendships; cross-sex romantic relationships, and marriage. Sociologists, they said, had tended to ignore many other ways in which people relate to each other. For instance, cross-sex or cross-age friendships; friendships between workmates; relationships between relatives (of the normal kind, that is, rather than those that tend to occur in Alabama); gay relationships, and extra-marital relationships.

Even in the late 1970s Huston and Levinger weren't entirely correct. There was lots of examination of both gay and extra-marital relationships. It was just that it was carried out by a very particular kind of sociologist known as a 'gossip columnist'. And of course a quarter of a century later their complaint is even less valid because a great deal of work has been done on the types of relationship they listed.

But refer to their complaint anyway. It contains the phrase 'extra-marital relationships', which always grabs everyone's imagination and will distract their attention from whichever argument you were losing.

Berscheid (1985)

Ellen Berscheid was another sociologist who highlighted the selective nature of her colleagues' research when it came to attraction. She drew their attention to the fact that an awful lot of the studies done on the subject had used as their sample group American college students. Berscheid seems to be correct in seeing this as a problem, in at least two respects. Firstly, American people may differ greatly from those in other societies and cultures. And secondly, college students are attracted to anything that's vaguely good-looking with a pulse. Or, if it's Freshers' Week, anything with a pulse.

Social Representations

Several sociologists have acknowledged that people have common perceptions about how relationships should be, rather than how they actually are. These are known as 'social representations', and can be a significant problem when conducting research. Respondents in a survey may well be inclined to provide an answer based on what they think their relationship should be like, instead of what it really is like. This certainly seems to be borne out by the facts. For instance, many people questioned in the course of research make the statement: 'I love my girlfriend.' Relatively few make the statement: 'For the last six months I've been sleeping with my girlfriend's sister.'

STARTING A RELATIONSHIP

In days gone by, relationships were simple. So simple, in fact, that there was only one way in which they started. He liked her; she liked him but was unable to say so and had to settle for smiling coyly at him; he wrote her a poem; she blushed at the poem's inevitable reference to flowers and bees; he asked her father for her hand in marriage; the physical relationship finally began after they had both made some promises to a man in a dress.

But modern relationships, being the complicated beasts they are, insist on having more energetic ways of getting started. Familiarity with these is crucial for anyone wanting to hold their own in a discussion about the subject.

E-mail Flirting

The workplace has always been a prime hunting ground for those in search of a relationship. But the flirting that is required to initiate contact with your partner of choice has to be undertaken with care. You don't want everyone in the office knowing that you find each other attractive. It could complicate your work relationships. It could lead to teasing and embarrassment. Or it could result in someone telling his wife.

So until the mid-1990s, office flirting tended to occur by the photocopier, or in the lift, or in the pub over drinks after work when you were the last two left. But the arrival of e-mail has led to a veritable explosion of flirting in offices up and down the land. Silent auctions of sexual intent can be engaged in by two people on opposite sides of an open-plan floor, their every word leading inexorably closer to the arrangement of a first date, which will in turn lead to the first kiss, which will in turn lead to rapturous carnal fulfilment. And all the time everyone else thinks you're processing invoices.

Internet Dating

This is the other great relationship innovation of the cyber age. Dating agencies used to be rather demure outfits, run by respectable women in twinsets who would only take you on their books if you were considered 'suitable'. But now the internet has taken over, hundreds of 'contacts' (a word that used only to be associated with journalists and batteries) are but a mouseclick away. Go to a dating web site, fill in a questionnaire about your appearance, your tastes and your sign of the Zodiac, then sit back and wait for the e-mails to come flooding in.

But beware. Most of the replies you receive will be junk e-mails, from people offering you guaranteed ways of making a million dollars on the Stock Market, or access to pictures of a highly graphic nature, or surgery to increase the size of certain parts of your anatomy. And even when replies are genuine, dangers abound. There are two main points you should bear in mind as you evaluate potential suitors:

1. **Hoodwinking**
   Most people tend to veer on the optimistic side when giving a physical description of themselves. It is entirely understandable that this should be so. Which of us, when we look in the mirror, does not choose to concentrate on those aspects of our appearance which are the most attractive, subconsciously blocking out those that are less appealing? But remember this when you read that someone

considers they have a 'hint of the young Bardot'. 'Hint' will probably be the operative word. In fact the similarities between them and the young Bardot may well begin and end with the fact that they both have the same number of limbs.

2. **Impersonating**
E-mail conversations do not take place in real time. Your suitor has time to think up each reply with which he or she aims to impress you. Consequently, as each bon mot tumbles into your in-box, wittily responding to your latest comment, you may form an impression of someone who is intelligent, erudite and charming. But how can you be sure that they will replicate this level of smartness in the flesh? How, indeed, can you be sure that the ideas are their own? They might have someone there with them, dictating each reply. You don't want this third party to be present on the date, do you, becoming part of the relationship? Or perhaps, depending on the nature of the web site, you do.

Lonely Hearts Columns

A more traditional method of starting relationships, but one which retains its popularity. Clearly the perils associated with internet dating can also apply, but they tend to be less marked. Unlike web sites, the press usually charges for placing ads. Charlatans and fantasists tend to blanch at the price of each line.

Lonely hearts columns have become ever more specialised. There are gay lonely hearts, pensioner's lonely hearts, gay pensioners' lonely hearts columns … the list is endless. Most of them, however, tend to rely on the same few abbreviations to minimise the cost. For instance:

WLTM stands for 'would like to meet'.
WSOH stands for 'wicked sense of humour'.
LTR stands for 'long-term relationship'.
TLC stands for 'tender, loving care'.
OHAC stands for 'own house and car'.

If you find yourself encountering 'GCH', this stands for 'gas central heating' and means that you've strayed into the property section by mistake.

Speed Dating

This is an activity which has become popular with young urban professionals. So busy do their high-powered jobs keep them that they don't have time to spend evening after evening going on lengthy dates in a search for their ideal partner. Instead they register with a speed dating firm, who organise parties of 30 or so people on their books. At these, everyone spends a very short time (typically three minutes) chatting to each of their prospective mates, so they can make a snap judgment on whether or not they want to arrange a more leisurely meeting in future.

Critics of speed dating ask how you can possibly decide if you are attracted to someone and want to become sexually involved with him or her in a period as short as three minutes. Male critics of speed dating ask what you're supposed to do with the spare two minutes and 59 seconds.

Dark Dating

This is similar to speed dating in the sense that the date is a group event organised for young professionals (by young professionals), but differs from it in that you spend all evening, rather than three minutes, with the people involved. The crucial factor is that you don't see any of them, because dark dating is exactly that – dating in the dark. You and a dozen or so other singletons pay for the privilege of enjoying a top-class meal in a top-class restaurant ... which has all its lights turned out. The waiters wear night-vision goggles so that they can see to serve you. It is not clear how you are meant to know where they are so you can make that little squiggle sign which means you want the bill.

The idea, claim the organisers, is that dark dating allows you to gain impressions of, and make impressions on, your fellow diners based purely on personality. The frivolous (as they would call them) matters of physical looks and dress sense are removed from the equation. We cannot recommend that you treat this phenomenon with anything other than amused contempt. You may formulate your objections along either or both of the following lines:

● **Theoretical**
It simply isn't true that people value intellect above appearance. An I.Q. of 150 is all very well, but that score is beaten as far as men are concerned by the number 38 (as in double-D) and, in women's minds, by the number 6 (as in pack). If anyone doubts this, ask them why it's George Clooney who sets women's pulses racing and not Bill Gates.

● **Practical**
It's just as well that the lights are out, as it means none of the other diners will be able to see the soup you've spilled down your shirt because the lights are out. The same will not be true, however, of all the people who see you on the way home.

Silent Dating

Dark dating removes visual clues to isolate aural ones; silent dating reverses the process. In this method, you are forbidden to speak to anyone else in the group, and instead have to communicate by passing notes. Graphologists would appear to hold an advantage here.

The thinking behind silent dating is that it challenges your ideas about self-expression. Deprived of your usual method of achieving it, you will consider much more carefully what you're 'saying' to a potential partner. It will also help avoid embarrassing verbal slips. For instance, the kind a woman may make when talking to a man with unusually prominent ears: 'I was doing the washing-up and nearly lost my ring down the lughole ... I mean, plughole.'

A disadvantage of this method of dating is that it's very hard to check for bad breath.

If you want to appear satirical, offer the thought that in getting partners to communicate only in writing, silent dating starts a relationship in exactly the way many of them end.

Supermarket Check-outs

Supermarkets used to fulfil only one role, that of a place where stressed women bought their weekly purchases while shouting at their badly behaved children. These days, when more and more people live on their own, one of their most important functions is to pair off single people who find themselves next to each other at the check-out.

There is, however, one simple rule that you should bear in mind as you size up potential partners. The way it's supposed to work is that you notice that the shopping of the good-looking man or woman behind you in the queue contains single-portion ready-meals, individual crème caramels, half-loaves of bread and other tell-tale signs of a solo lifestyle. If all they've got in their basket are 17 tins of cat food and a Stephen King novel, it may be advisable to give them a wide berth.

Other Methods of Dating

If those who you are bluffing have already heard of speed dating, dark dating and so on, maintain your upper hand by throwing into the conversation 'astro-dating' and 'bio-rhythm dating'. These two terms provide excellent BPS (Bluff Per Syllable) value. Simply by naming them you not only explain how they work, you also reveal how risible they are.

ENDING A RELATIONSHIP

It is a sad but inescapable truth that relationships sometimes come to an end. This can happen despite the best efforts of both parties involved: making more effort to understand each other, taking an interest in your partner's hobbies, making sure that your husband is asleep before you go and telephone your lover from the spare room.

There are only three groups of people with a professional interest in the termination of a complete stranger's relationship: sociologists, divorce lawyers, and the manufacturers of microwave meals-for-one. Of these, sociologists are perhaps the most loathsome.

Studies of how relationships end have covered the factors which can cause it to happen, and the ways in which the people involved deal with the situation. As a would-be expert you will be expected to show an awareness of both areas of work. Indeed, when you are obliged to conduct the inevitable post mortem on the demise of a relationship, assuring the forlorn one that such situations have happened since time immemorial may offer a crumb of comfort.

The Causes of Relationship Breakdown

Linear and Curvilinear Models

These are two theories about the level of happiness as a marriage progresses. Both are based on empirical research. The fact that they come to different conclusions proves yet again that in whichever direction your bluffing carries you, there will always be a study on hand to back you up.

The **linear model** states that the level of marital happiness is high in the early years, then decreases steadily as the marriage wears on. It was first put forward in 1961. Further evidence was provided in 1969 in a study compiled by Blood and Wolfe. The names say it all, really.

The **curvilinear model**, advanced by W.R. Burr in 1960, states that marital happiness decreases towards the middle years of a marriage, but then rises again in the later years. There are many explanations for why this may be so. We recommend that you stick to a relatively cynical one. For instance that the level of marital happiness nosedives when the children are born, then rises again when they clear off.

Deception

Several studies have been conducted into the effects on relationships of deception. A basic piece of work in this area is that of Miller, Mogeau and Sleight. They found that relationships change dramatically if one partner is discovered to be engaged in duplicitous behaviour about a serious matter. Clearly Sleight and co. knew a thing or two.

An intriguing fact about deceit was discovered by Mark Comadena in 1982. People in close relationships, it was found, were less able to tell when their partners were deceiving them than those in new relationships that were still developing. When referring to this study, the advanced bluffer can adopt a cunning ploy: accept that these were indeed the apparent results of Comadena's study, but question whether they were the real results. Yes, you can say, it may be true that the middle-aged wife has failed to spot the inconsistencies in her husband's story that he was playing golf with friends on the Wednesday night in question, an error she would not have made when they were both 19. Then again it may not. It may be the case that she's fully aware of which hotel he was in and with whom, but as he's now earning four times the salary he was at 19 she's prepared to turn a blind eye to it.

Novelty

An important aspect in the breakdown of many relationships is novelty. If the partners cease to gain stimulation from being together, they are much more likely to split up. Duck and Miell (1986) found that respondents in their study often said a relationship had broken down because it 'wasn't going anywhere'. There is further support for this theory from another

47

quarter. 'Not going anywhere' is the reason that many commuters cite for the breakdown of their relationship with modern train companies.

Physical Separation

This is another factor commonly cited as a cause of relationships ending. Shaver, Furman and Burmester (1985) found that 46% of pre-college relationships ended after one partner went away to study. Given the well-known propensities of college students, we can only surmise that the other 54% must have been exceptionally unattractive.

Duck (1988)

Steve Duck (it's that man again) studied marriages over a wide cross-section of society to establish the factors which made it more likely that a couple would be unhappy or even divorce. He found five sorts of marriage that were statistically prone to weakness:

1. Marriages in which the partners were younger than average.

2. Marriages in which the partners were from lower socio-economic groups.

3. Marriages between partners from different demographic backgrounds (race, religion, etc.).

4. Marriages between people whose parents had got divorced.

5. Marriages between people who had a higher than average number of pre-marital sexual partners.

You might care to suggest that Duck has missed the vital advice offered by Charlie Watts from his own experience. While other members of the Rolling Stones have engaged in a lifelong pursuit of sampling relationships, their drummer has been happily married to his wife Shirley since the tender age of 23. Watts' piece of wisdom on the subject is that the secret of a successful marriage is separate bathrooms.

Patterns of Relationship Breakdown

So the relationship is ending. It isn't simply the case that you shout at him for three hours, storm off to your mother's, come back to collect all your stuff two days later when you know he won't be there, then leave for the final time having dialled the Australian speaking clock and left the phone off the hook. Or rather, of course, it is. But this isn't the bit relationship experts are interested in. (They really don't know what they're missing.) Their area of study is how the final stages of the relationship are played out, how both parties deal with, and react to, the prospect of splitting up. There are several views of the way this happens.

Rusbult (1987)

Caryl Rusbult examined the strategies couples use to cope with dissatisfaction in their relationship. She found that they were divided into four categories:

- **Exit strategies**: people get out of the relationship, either literally or at least mentally, i.e., they think about leaving.

- **Voice strategies**: people discuss their problems.

- **Loyalty strategies**: people wait for things to get better, hoping that the problem will sort itself out.

- **Neglect strategies**: people do nothing to tackle the issue, they simply let the relationship crumble.

It should be noted that the final two categories could very easily be mistaken for each other. You can imagine the scene: the couple sit watching television together, barely a word having passed between them for hours.

> He turns to her: 'Excuse me for asking, dear, but is that a neglect strategy you're employing there?'
> 'Oh no, darling. I can see why you say that, but it's definitely a loyalty strategy.'
> 'Ah, I see. Just checking.'

Noller (1985)

Patricia Noller identified a stage that couples often pass through at the end of a relationship, which she labelled the 'negativity cycle'. In this the partners complain about each other without really addressing their underlying concerns. They avoid proper discussion, and concentrate instead on 'scoring points' off each other. In particularly sour relationships 'scoring points' can become 'bouncing dinner plates'.

Duck's Four-stage Model (1988)

Yet another contribution from Duck. You would expect such a seasoned and prolific performer to supply in-depth analysis, employing meticulous logic and complex jargon. Nor would you be disappointed. Duck sets a perfect example to the single-minded bluffer: explain everything, and use very big words:

1. **The intra-psychic phase**
   This is the kind of language you should be striving for. 'Intra-psychic' – four syllables, a hyphen in the middle, and one of the words is in Latin. Wonderful work. What it actually means is that one partner is beginning to have doubts, thinking to themselves about the possibility of the relationship ending.

2. **The dyadic phase**
   This is when the first person communicates their doubts to the other partner, and there is a discussion about the possibility of breaking up. A reconciliation may be attempted, but if that is not possible, the process moves on to phase three.

3. **The social phase**
   This is the stage at which the couple work out the practical consequences that will result from their relationship ending, and inform close friends and family. It is also the stage at which her mother says 'I told you so.'

4. **The grave-dressing phase**
   It is at this point that the relationship finally ends, and each partner goes on to give their own version of the break-up to friends and family. For instance, he blames the increasing divergence in outlook and interests that was a regrettable but inevitable result of two people maturing and developing in different directions, while she tells everyone about the purple bra she found in his briefcase.

Effects of Relationship Termination

When a relationship comes to an end, the effects on the people involved can vary widely. There is, for instance, the realisation that you're totally on your own; no-one to talk to when you get home from work, no-one to listen to as they tell you about their day, no-one except yourself to buy gifts for at Christmas. But it's not all good news. Some of the effects of a relationship ending can be extremely negative.

A study conducted in 1992, for instance, reviewed the results from a selection of surveys, and found that people in disrupted relationships were more susceptible than others of the same sex and age group to heart disease, alcoholism, drug dependency and sleep disturbances. While Ray Cochrane (1983, 1996) found that the divorced were five and a half times more likely than the married to be admitted to a mental hospital. Although whether it's worse to find yourself in a marriage or in a mental hospital could be seen as a matter of opinion.

It is commonly accepted by relationship experts that there is a gender element to the negative effects of marriage breakdown. For women, the stage at which they're most likely to suffer from depression is before divorce, when the marriage is in trouble. While for men, depression tends to come after the divorce, when they realise for the first time how much they depended on their partner for happiness and peace of mind. During the marriage itself, he saw his wife not as an emotional support, but as that person who always insisted on doing the vacuuming when he was trying to watch football on TV. While she saw him as the one who failed to realise that a rubbish bin ever needed to be emptied.

If the discussion becomes too depressing, you can

rescue it by mentioning John Cleese's theory on the matter. The Monty Python star has had three wives and says that the end of a marital relationship is nothing to be ashamed of, claiming that he would rather be married seven times to seven interesting women than once to someone who bored him. His divorce lawyers wholeheartedly agree with him.

RELATIONSHIPS AROUND THE WORLD

Many people in the Western world assume that their customs regarding relationships are universally true. They take it for granted that some things are the natural, never-ending way of the world. That relationships are expected to be monogamous, for example. That children will be raised by their biological parents. That divorce lawyers drive Ferraris.

But many countries conduct their relationships in ways which are radically different from Western norms. It is worth taking on board a few of these, as they will give your bluffing a certain world-weariness, and enable you to appear wise and well travelled.

Tibetan Polyandry

Polyandry is the act of a woman having two or more husbands. It is very rare indeed, so knowing that it takes place in Tibet will be your bluffing equivalent of serving a particular sort of caviar that is only produced by one tiny village in a remote part of Russia. Except cheaper.

Not only do Tibetans practise polyandry, they practise 'fraternal polyandry' – the woman marries two or more brothers. As a result, her brother-in-law is also her husband, her uncle is also her father, her daughter is also her niece... Not even *Eastenders* gets this complicated.

Matrilineal Societies

Almost all societies around the world are 'patrilineal'. In other words, descent is traced through the male line. But there have been one or two examples of 'matrilineal' societies, where the women have been in control. One such was the society of the Nayar in southern India, which existed in the early years of British colonialism. The Nayar women took exclusive responsibility for the upbringing of their children. The only role of the biological father was to impregnate the woman. After this he would have nothing further to do with her.

This tradition is being revived on many housing estates the world over.

Milk Siblings

In many Islamic societies, children who have been given milk by the same woman are known as 'milk siblings', and are treated as if they were real siblings. Male and female milk siblings are therefore prohibited from marrying.

Coincidentally, there is a tradition in Britain of children borne by women on the same milk-round looking like each other, almost as though they had the same father.

Closely Defined Relationships

Some societies are very exact when it comes to defining their relationships. The Polish, for example, have two separate words for 'uncle': your father's brother is your 'stryj', while your mother's brother is your 'wuj'. Winning Scrabble scores in Poland have been known to reach the low millions.

Keeping It in the Family

A male Orthodox Jew is expected to marry his deceased brother's widow. Also, some Islamic societies expect a man to marry his father's brother's daughter; this is done as a way of ensuring that property remains within the family. It also has the welcome side-effect that guests at the wedding always know someone they can talk to.

Twenty per cent of marriages around the world are between first cousins, including Albert Einstein and Charles Darwin. However, in half of the United States and in China such marriages are taboo. Genetic research reveals that the closer the parental relationship, the greater the risk of birth defects or genetic disorder for their children. A child of unrelated parents has a risk of around 2–3%, and the risk rises to 4–6% for children of first cousins without a family history of genetic disorders. For children of first degree relatives – such as parent and child, or brother and sister – it increases to about 30% (including the risk of death).

This may explain the demise of the ancient Pharaohs where brother married sister or father married daughter when no-one else was royal enough. In Roman Egypt marriages between siblings were common. The father was usually in favour of this as it meant one less meal to pay for at the reception.

Arranged Marriages

Arranged marriages are widely known about by Westerners, but what is less well known (and this, therefore, is where your bluffing can come into its own) is how successful they often are. Such marriages receive a fairly bad press in the West, but most studies conducted in societies which originated the custom show how stable they can be.

Gupta and Singh (1992), for instance, compared couples in India who had married freely with those who had taken part in arranged marriages. The latter reported that their feelings of love continued to grow as the relationship progressed, while those who wed freely experienced reduced feelings after five years.

Another point to make which few people recognise about arranged marriages is how common they are in the West, not among members of ethnic minorities but among the indigenous population. Your audience will probably express surprise when you mention this. Tell them to find the daughter of a well-to-do couple who tried to get her own way on her wedding dress, reception venue or (in extreme cases) choice of groom, and ask her about the term 'arranged marriage'.

Trobriand Pregnancies

The Trobriand tribe in Australia were an aboriginal group studied by sociologists in the 1890s. They had the curious theory that sex and pregnancy were entirely unrelated to each other. Instead they believed that the baby was created by a spirit that entered through the woman's ear. Some *Star Wars* fans are of the opinion that Princess Leia was related to the Trobriand tribe and was scared of getting pregnant. Nothing else could explain that ridiculous hairdo.

Of course there is still a sizeable aboriginal community in Australia, and their relationship customs continue to provide material for the bluffer. What they call their 'marriage groups' are of particular interest, not least because of the splendid names involved. Each child is born into a particular group, and this determines which other group he or she must marry into when they become an adult. For instance, a male Panunga must marry a female Purula. When they have a child, of whichever sex, it will be an Appungerta. Conversely, a male Purula has to marry a female Panunga. Their children will belong to the Kumara group. An Appungerta has to marry an Umbitchana. Their child will be a Panunga.

This system, you can explain, has two advantages. It keeps in place a rigid societal structure that shows respect for the past. And it fosters great confidence because, after working out which group you're in, any other problem life can throw at you is a piece of cake.

Differences within the Western World

It may not always be possible (or if possible then advisable) to focus your 'relationships around the world' bluffing exclusively on non-Western societies. People occasionally like to return to more familiar territory, to discuss matters from their own experience. It would not do for you to develop a reputation as one who knows all about the Indian Toda (q.v.) but nothing about your own back yard. We suggest that you ready yourself with a few choice comments from the French anthropologist Raymonde Carroll. Her husband, also an anthropologist, is American. This prompted her to publish (in 1988) *Cultural Misunderstandings: The French-American Experience*.

Some of her most interesting observations concern the different ways in which French and American couples behave when in public. In France, if a couple meet up with a group of friends, it has to be shown that the group relationship takes priority. This may be achieved, for instance, by everyone making little jokes at the expense of the partner with whom they are less familiar. There is no malice involved, simply a need to demonstrate that the couple's relationship doesn't threaten ties with the rest of the group.

Behaviour towards each other is also a factor. French couples are perfectly happy to argue in front of their colleagues, seeing no problem with airing differences in this way. But Americans would interpret such actions as a threat to their relationship, tantamount to admitting in front of their friends that the relationship was in trouble.

Extra-Marital Sex

Always a winner. Just mentioning the words will guarantee you the undivided attention of everyone present.

Extra-marital sex is, of course, frowned upon in the West, the frown being worn by everyone except the two people having the relationship. But there are cultures where it is perfectly acceptable. For instance W.H.R. Rivers (1906) studied the Toda of the southern Deccan plateau of India (great bluffing material, this – a century old, and from somewhere no-one's ever heard of). In this society, a man was expected to allow his wife to have an affair with another man if she asked. The fact that the women were the ones who had affairs is unfortunate for Western husbands in search of an excuse to be unfaithful. Nevertheless, it might be worth asking your wife anyway. Try presenting it in a very academic light, throwing in an occasional "What's sauce for the goose ..."

GLOSSARY

Attraction – what two people must first establish before a relationship can even begin. (There are people who do not agree with this, but they are known as 'stalkers'.)

body language – non-verbal communication between two people signified by a variety of movements, many of them completely subconscious, and shown by studies to tally 80% of the total. After a few years of marriage this figure can rise to 100%.

bundling – custom in which unmarried lovers sleep together wearing their clothes, so that they can assess their suitability for each other without having sex. At least that's what they tell their parents.

bunny-boiler – a woman who over-reacts to being shunned by a man. Derives from the 1987 film *Fatal Attraction* in which Glenn Close gains revenge on Michael Douglas by cooking his child's pet rabbit.

Coolidge effect – the ability of a man to become sexually aroused when presented with a fresh partner, even though he is exhausted after intercourse with his last one. The term derives from a visit to a chicken farm by the U.S. President Calvin Coolidge. His wife asked the farmer how many times a day a cock could mount a hen. 'About forty,' came the reply. Mrs. Coolidge said: 'Please tell that to my husband.' The farmer duly did so, and in return was asked by the President whether the cock always mounted the same hen. 'No,' said the farmer, 'it's a different hen every time.' Coolidge said: 'Please tell that to my wife.'

DADT – 'Don't ask, don't tell', a policy recommended for relationships. This was the policy adopted by the U.S. army in which recruits are not asked whether they have engaged in homosexual activity, and are expected not to volunteer the information either. In civilian usage the term has widened to include the question of whether or not you have committed adultery. The practice began during Bill Clinton's presidency, which is ironic, as the man himself seems to have had an imperfect understanding of it: he didn't tell even when he was asked.

doused lights – a group sex game (so-called because it takes place in the dark). Originated by the Inuit. They have to do something to keep warm.

endogamy – the act of marrying a relative. Frowned on in most cultures, although if you're a member of the British aristocracy you probably have little choice.

flirting – an indication of sexual interest ranging from subtle eye signals to full frontal assault.

gay relationship – that between two members of the same sex. The numbers of gay men and women (according to most reliable surveys) are perhaps lower than many people would think. Between 3–4% of men are homosexuals. Only 1% of women are lesbians. It is curious how many of them feel the need to write letters to *Penthouse* giving full and frank accounts of their experiences.

homogamy – not, as you might expect, a slang term for monogamy in homosexual relationships but the act of marrying someone of a similar age, race, religion, level of education, etc. to yourself.

Horney, Karen – psychoanalyst who followed in Freud's footsteps. For those seeking the status of instant expert, a name like this provides a real bonus: effort-free bluffing. All you have to do is mention it, then sit back while everyone provides their own punchline.

LAT – Living Apart Together; maintaining separate residences and an intimate relationship. Suggest that the latter is sustained by the former. Apart from the fact that the physical space inherent in the arrangement allows greater emotional space, it's more difficult to keeps tabs on each other.

Lupercalia – a Roman festival which took place on the 15th February, and which some see as the origin of Valentine's Day. During the festival, women who sought fertility would be lashed with fresh strips of goatskin by naked or semi-naked young men. Perhaps some of them still do.

marriage gradient – the tendency for men to marry women who are slightly younger, smaller and of lower status than they are. Other people also see marriage in terms of a slope, although in their case it is in conjunction with the word 'slippery'.

metacommunication – the act of talking with your partner not about the problems in your relationship, but about the problems you have with the way you talk about the problems in your relationship. The aim of this is to prevent your discussions from descending into slanging matches. Coming soon: **metametacommunication**, in which you talk about the problems you have with the way you talk about the problems you have with the way you talk about the problems in your relationship.

monogamy – the state of remaining sexually faithful to one partner. Or, if you ask a man, something used to make furniture.

MSO – My Significant Other; politically correct term for spouse or partner. A good line to take is to question the implication of its middle word. 'The person one loves more than anyone or anything in the whole world' is indeed significant. But then so is an earthquake.

polyandrous marriage – that undertaken by a woman who already has one or more husbands. This is almost a definition of the phrase 'triumph of hope over experience'.

polygamous marriage – that undertaken by a man who already has one or more wives. See also 'glutton' and 'punishment'.

POSSLQs: term used by the U.S. Department of the Census to denote a cohabiting couple. It stands for 'persons of the opposite sex sharing living quarters'. Oh the romance of it.

seven-year itch – the time when partners in a relationship are traditionally thought to become dissatisfied with it. There is also the seven-day itch, but this is a medical problem often experienced shortly after relationships of a single night's duration.

sexual exclusivity – means the same as 'monogamy'. Yet another term for this is 'fidelity'. Women keep inventing words for it in the hope that men will one day understand what it means.

THE AUTHOR

Mark Mason has had many important relationships in his life. Among the most acrimonious have been those with his bank manager and the Inland Revenue, while the least rewarding has been that with Coventry City Football Club. Perhaps the most enduring relationship of his life has been that with sticky toffee pudding.

As far as romantic relationships are concerned, none of Mason's girlfriends has ever had a single complaint about his behaviour in any respect whatsoever. Apart from the fact that he's a pathological liar.

THE BLUFFER'S® GUIDES

The three million-copy best-selling humour series that contains facts, jargon and inside information – all you need to know to hold your own among experts.

Available from all good bookshops, online, or direct from the publisher: in the U.K. (0)207 582 7123 (post free), and in the U.S.A. 1-800-243-0495 (toll free).

www.bluffers.com